HBJ BOOKMARK READING PROGRAM, EAGLE EDITION

Margaret Early

Elizabeth K. Cooper

Nancy Santeusanio

Level 6

World of Surprises

- WORLD OF SURPRISES
  PEOPLE AND PLACES

HARCOURT BRACE JOVANOVICH, PUBLISHERS

New York   Chicago   San Francisco   Atlanta   Dallas   and   London

ACKNOWLEDGMENTS: For permission to reprint copyrighted material, grateful acknowledgment is made to the following sources:

Follett Publishing Company: Adapted from *Nobody Listens to Andrew* by Elizabeth Guilfoile (retitled: "No One Listens to Andrew"). Copyright © 1957 by Follett Publishing Company, a division of Follett Corporation.
Grosset & Dunlap, Inc.: Adapted from *The Little Duck Said Quack, Quack, Quack* by Grace and Olive Barnett (retitled: "Isabel Quacks"). Copyright © 1955 by Grosset & Dunlap, Inc. Adapted from *How to Find a Friend* by Sara Asheron. Copyright © 1964 by Sara Asheron.
Harcourt Brace Jovanovich, Inc.: *Timothy Turtle* (abridged and adapted) by Alice Vaught Davis, copyright © 1940, by Harcourt Brace Jovanovich, Inc.; renewed, 1968 by Joseph C. Gill. "We rowed into fog . . ." by Shiki from *Cricket Songs: Japanese Haiku*, translated and © 1964 by Harry Behn.
Highlights for Children Inc., Columbus, Ohio: "A New Friend" by Marjorie Allen Anderson from *Children's Activities*, 1950. Copyright Children's Activities.
Alfred A. Knopf, Inc.: "Sea Calm" from *Selected Poems* by Langston Hughes. Copyright 1926 by Alfred A. Knopf, Inc. and renewed 1954 by Langston Hughes.
Little, Brown and Co.: "The Camel" from *Verses From 1929 On* by Ogden Nash. Copyright 1933 by Ogden Nash.
McIntosh and Otis, Inc.: "At the Zoo" from *Whispers and Other Poems* by Myra Cohn Livingston. Copyright © 1958 by Myra Cohn Livingston.
Parents' Magazine Enterprises, Inc.: "The Elephant on the Bus" by Rube Rosen from *Humpty Dumpty's Magazine*. Copyright © 1958 by Humpty Dumpty, Inc., a division of Parents' Magazine Enterprises, Inc.
G. P. Putnam's Sons: "The Seals" from *Hop, Skip and Jump* by Dorothy Aldis. Copyright 1934 by Dorothy Aldis, renewed.
Karen S. Solomon: "Upon the Beach" from *Funday* by Ilo Orleans. "Lost in the Zoo" from *I Watch the World Go By* by Ilo Orleans. Published by Henry Z. Walck.
Arnold Spilka: "The Talking Tiger" from *A Lion I Can Do Without* by Arnold Spilka. Copyright © 1964 by Arnold Spilka.

Ellen Appleby: 148–155; Marilyn Bass: 70–72, 83; Kevin Callahan: 138–139; Jim Cummins: 98–103; Doug Cuchman: 104–111; Ray Cruz: 49–53; Renée Daily: 74–78, 84–87; Bert Dodson: 25–30; Len Ebert: 88–93; Judith Fast: 188–189; Arthur Friedman: 20–24; Shelley Freshman: 194–208; Jürg Furrer: 112–118; John Hamberger: 140–145; Fred Harsh: 66–69, 79–82; Ron Himler: 170–178; Robin Hotchkiss: 31, 32, 62–64, 94–96, 126–128, 158–160, 190–192; Phyllis Luch: 7, 33, 65, 97, 129, 161, 194; John Melo/Fran Stiles: 54–61; Sal Murdocca: 119–125; Roger Paré: 179–187; Ruth Sanderson: 131–137, 162–169; Steven Schindler: 209–221; Emanuel Schongut: 8; Judith Strick: 130; Maggie Swanson: 41; Lorna Tomei: 15–19; Joseph Veno: 73.

HBJ PHOTOS: Page 9; 10; 11; 12; 13; 14; 74; 77

Page 24, John M. Burnley/Bruce Coleman; 35, Bill Meng, © New York Zoological Society; 36, Tom McHugh/Photo Researchers; 37, Jerry Cooke/Animals Animals; 38, George Hall/Woodfin Camp; 39, Tom McHugh/Photo Researchers; 40, © New York Zoological Society; 42, Diane Wayman; 43, Stan Wayman; 44, Stan Wayman; 45, Stan Wayman/Photo Researchers; 46, Russ Kinne/Photo Researchers; 47, Fran Allan/Animals Animals; 48, Stan Wayman; 75, Earl Roberge/Photo Researchers; 76, J. Alex Langley/DPI; 78, UPI; 146, © 1978 Museum of Fine Arts, Boston, M. & M. Karolik Collection; 147, Sekai Bunka; 157, Lida Moser/DPI.

Contents

New Friends

(To be read by the teacher.)

A New Friend

They've taken in the furniture;
I watched carefully.
I wondered, "Will there be a child
Just right to play with me?"

So I peeked through the garden fence.
(I couldn't wait to see.)
I found the little boy next door
Was peeking back at me.

MARJORIE ALLEN ANDERSON

8

Finding a Friend

by SARA ASHERON

Benny was not happy.

He had just moved into a new house.

He liked the house.

But he had no friends here.

All he had was his dog, Rex.

"I'll never find a friend," he said.

"Oh well, I can play with Rex."

Benny called, "Here Rex, here boy!"

But Rex did not come.

"Oh, no," said Benny, "Rex is lost!"

9

Benny ran down the street.
"Here, Rex!" he called again.

A boy came across the street.
He went up to Benny.
"Did your dog run away?" he asked.

"No," said Benny, "we just moved
here and Rex got lost."

"My name is Carlos," said the boy.
"Do you want me to help you look
for him?"

"Yes, thanks," said Benny.

10

"Let's look down this next street,"
said Carlos.

"Dogs like to dig in the lot."

They walked to the next street.

Benny saw a boy and girl across the
street, but no Rex.

Carlos called, "Ruth and Bobby, this
is Benny.

He cannot find his dog."

The boy and girl looked up and
down the street.

Then they ran across.

"We will help you look," said Ruth.

"Let's look for him at the school," said Bobby.

"Dogs like to play by the school."

So they all went to the next street.

Benny saw a girl across the street, but no Rex.

Ruth called, "Rosa, this is Benny. He cannot find his dog."

"I'll help you look," said Rosa.

The children walked down to the next street.

They looked and looked for Rex.

All at once, Benny stopped.
"That is my new house!" he cried.

"Then I live across the street from you," said Carlos.

"So do we," said Bobby, "in that house with the white door."

"And I live in that house by the big tree," said Rosa.

Benny was very surprised.
"Say," cried Benny, "I have a tree by the garden in back of my house.
It looks good for climbing.
Let's climb on it!"

They all ran to Benny's house.
Then Benny stopped and laughed.
He saw Rex, playing with two dogs.
"Well, look at that," said Carlos.
"Your dog has some new friends."

Benny looked at the children.
"I have new friends, too," he said.
Then he said, "Come on!"
And they all ran over to climb in
Benny's tree.

A Penny a Day

Ann lived with her grandfather and grandmother.

One night at supper, Ann said, "Please help me.

I have to remember to take a penny to school tomorrow.

I'll need a penny a day from now on."

"A penny for what?" asked Grandfather.

"It is a surprise," said Ann.
"It has something to do with elephants."

"Oh, elephants," said Grandmother.

Ann liked elephants.

In her room she had many of them.

She had elephant pictures that she had painted in school.

She had elephants she had made.

Ann had books, too.

The ones she liked best had pictures of real elephants in them.

"One day I'll see a real elephant," Ann said.

"One day I'll **own** a real elephant!"

Many days went by.

Ann painted pictures of elephants.

She got new elephant books.

And she remembered to take her penny a day to school.

One afternoon Ann came home with a note.

She gave it to Grandmother.

"It has something to do with the big surprise," said Ann.

"All the children in my school are going on a bus.

You and Grandfather can come and see the big surprise."

17

The next morning, a bus came to get the children.

Many other people got on the bus with them.

The bus stopped at a park.

Ann was the first to jump down.

"Look!" she called.

"Now you can see the surprise."

Grandmother and Grandfather **were** surprised.

"I own a real elephant at last," said Ann.

"What do you think of her?"

"It is a real elephant," said Grandfather.

"But, Ann, you cannot own a real elephant like this."

Ann's teacher laughed.

"Ann owns some of the elephant," he said.

"Look at what it says."

This is Penny. Many children gave a penny a day to help get her for the city park. A girl who likes elephants named her "Penny."

"I am that girl!" said Ann with a happy laugh.

19

No One Listens to Andrew

by ELIZABETH GUILFOILE

ANDREW: Mother, Mother!

MOTHER: Wait, Andrew. I must say good-by to Mrs. Parks. She must get the bus before dark.

ANDREW: Dad, Dad! I saw something in my room!

FATHER: Wait, Andrew. I must cut the grass before dark.

ANDREW: Ruth, Ruth! I saw something in my room. It was on my bed.

RUTH: Wait, Andrew. I must get my skates. I want to skate before dark.

ANDREW: Bobby, Bobby! I saw something in my room. It was on my bed by the window.

BOBBY: Please, Andrew. I must find my bat and ball. I want to play before dark.

ANDREW: Listen, Mr. Neighbor. I saw something in my room. It was on my bed by the window. It was big and it was black.

MR. NEIGHBOR: Not now, Andrew. I must take my dog for a walk before dark.

ANDREW: Listen, Mother. Listen, Dad. Listen, Ruth. Listen, Bobby. Listen, Mr. Neighbor. I SAW A BEAR ON MY BED!

MOTHER: Call an officer!

FATHER: Call a firefighter!

BOBBY: Call a dog catcher!

RUTH: Call the zoo!

MR. NEIGHBOR: I will! I will!

MOTHER: Look! It is by the window.

FATHER: Look! It is big and black!

BOBBY: Look! It is on Andrew's bed!

RUTH: Look! It is a bear. Andrew said it was a bear. But no one listens to Andrew.

DOG CATCHER: It is a nice gentle bear.

FIREFIGHTER: It climbed up the tree. It climbed in the window!

ZOO WOMAN: It is dry in the woods. This bear was looking for water. I will take this bear to the zoo.

FATHER: Next time, we will listen to Andrew!

What Next?

May lived on Main Street.
No children lived around her.
It was very quiet all the time.
May said to her mother, "It is too quiet around here."

Her mother said, "Just wait, May. Tomorrow it will not be quiet."

The next day, May was reading.
She heard something.
Two trucks came up Main Street.
May ran out to look.

People jumped down from the trucks.

They went into a lot across from May's house.

They went to work, cutting the grass and digging holes in the lot.

May ran back into the house.

"People are working across the way!" she said.

Then she heard something new.
"What next?" said May.

"Go see," said her mother.

May ran out the door just in time to
see a big bulldozer coming up the street.

It went to the lot and got to work.

"A real bulldozer!" said May.

"What next?"

Then she heard something.

R-r-r-r-r-r!

A car came up Main Street.

It stopped, and two officers got out.

"Out of the way.

Please stay out of the way,"
they said.

"What next?" said May.

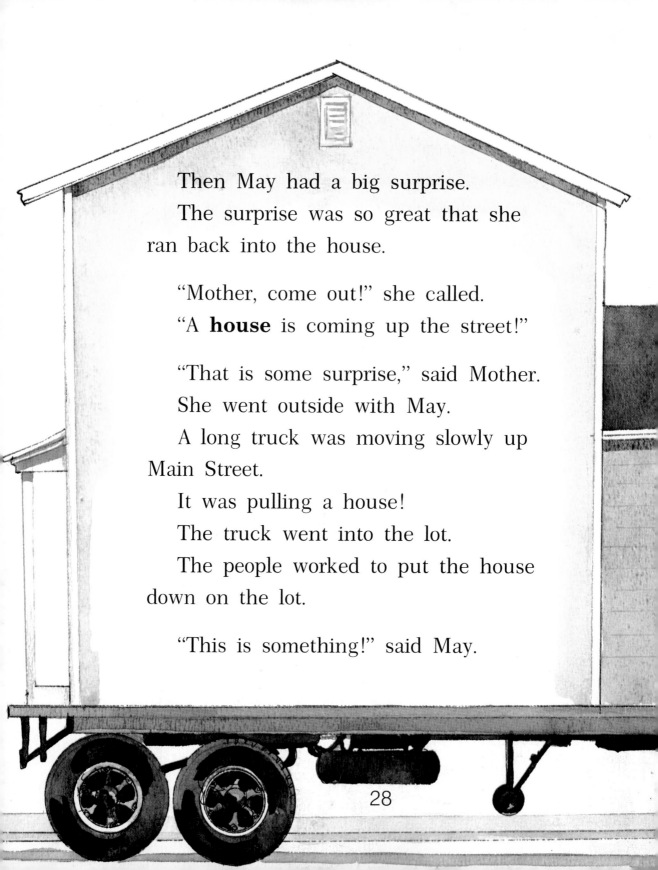

Then May had a big surprise.
The surprise was so great that she
ran back into the house.

"Mother, come out!" she called.
"A **house** is coming up the street!"

"That is some surprise," said Mother.
She went outside with May.
A long truck was moving slowly up
Main Street.
It was pulling a house!
The truck went into the lot.
The people worked to put the house
down on the lot.

"This is something!" said May.

All morning long, May sat and looked at the people working on the house.

At last they went away.

May went back inside.

"The street is not quiet today," she said to her mother.

"What next?"

May heard a knock at the door.

"Go see who it is, May," said Mother.

It was a boy and a girl.

The boy said, "My name is Ray.

This is Maria.

We live in the new house.

Can you come out and play?"

"Oh, yes," said May, "but I have to tell Mother first."

She ran back and told her mother.

May's mother laughed.

"That is great!" she said.

And the street was never too quiet for May after that.

Do You Get the Picture?

Look at each part of the picture. Tell what each part is about. Put the picture parts together to find the main idea of all the pictures. What tells about all of the picture?

1. A girl is jumping rope.
2. A girl catches the ball.
3. The children are playing.

A story has a main idea, too. The main idea is the one thing that most of the sentences are about. Find the main idea in this story.

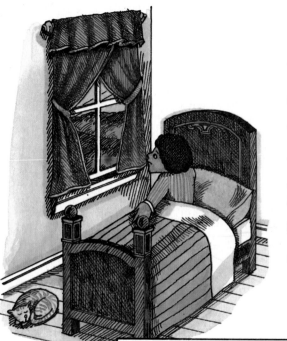

It's no fun to be sick when friends are playing outside. Jan was in bed with a cold. From her window she saw Kim and Jack playing. Jan was sad. She wanted to go out and play, too.

Try This

1. Which sentence tells the main idea?

2. How are the other sentences like the picture parts on page 31?

3. Is the main idea like a picture part or like the whole picture?

Animals
All Around

Wild Animals
in the City

Where can you find wild animals in the city? Try going to the city zoo.

The zoo animals have come from many parts of the world. Some, like the bear, are from cold lands. Some, like the elephant, come from hot lands.

In some zoos, the animals have lots of room. They live the way they did in the wild.

Zoo animals need many things. Bears need dark homes to lie in on hot days. The elephant needs water to drink and splash on its back.

Some animals might need trees to
live in. Some might need ponds to play
in. And some might need grass to eat
and sleep on.

This zoo has cages. They are like
little rooms for the animals. They have
back doors so the animals can go outside.
The animals can go out in the sun. But
they can come in again if it gets cold
and wet.

Many animals have happy homes in the zoo. They get the food they need. They do not have to hunt for it. Some of the food comes from far away.

People like to come and see the hungry animals eating.

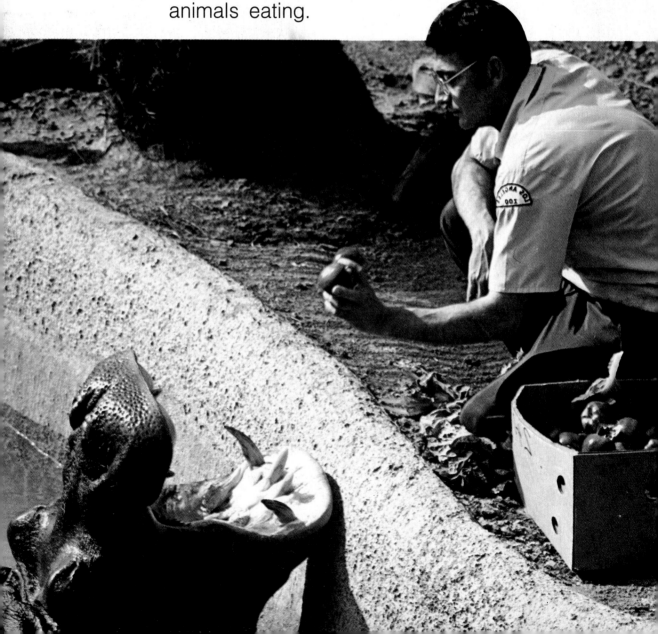

It takes lots of work to run a zoo.
Many people are needed to do it.

The animals need the right food.
They can get sick. Then they have to
be looked after. They need good
homes to live in. And the zoo has to
be cleaned day after day.

Why do people go to zoos? They like to see beautiful wild animals. Most people cannot go to the lands of the wild animals. So a city builds a zoo and brings the animals to the people.

(To be read by the teacher.)

At the Zoo

I've been to the zoo
    where the thing that you do
    is watching the things
    that the animals do —

and watching
    the animals
    all watching
        you!

MYRA COHN LIVINGSTON

41

PANDAS

by GRACE MOREMEN

What animal is this? It looks like a bear with big black boots. But it is not a bear at all. It is called a panda.

A panda is a wild animal. It comes from China. You can see pandas in some zoos in America.

What do you think a panda looks like when it is little? You can see in the picture. The panda is very, very little.

The panda gets big fast. Soon it looks more like a bear. When it grows older, the panda lives away from the mother. In zoos, the pandas live 14 years or more.

What do pandas like to do? They
like to play. Look at the picture. Pandas
like to roll over. They roll faster and
faster. They go right over grass and
little logs.

Pandas like to climb, too. Then they
jump down and roll over. They get up
and do it again. Pandas are a funny
sight when they are playing.

Pandas are wild animals. They might look like little bears. But they have big teeth. You can see the panda's teeth in this picture.

Why do pandas have big teeth? They need them for the plants they eat. In the wild, pandas eat plants that grow around them. In the zoo, they get to eat softer food, too.

After they eat, pandas like to sleep.
Some pandas sleep on their backs. Some
sleep all rolled up. And some sleep
sitting up!

Pandas live in the cold parts of China.
They like the snow. But they do not like
hot days.

It is a hot summer day at the zoo. The panda looks down into the cold water. She jumps in. Oh, it is nice and cold! She plays and splashes, just as girls and boys do in summer.

It must be fun to be a panda. What do you think?

The Seals

The seals all flap
Their shining flips
And bounce balls on
Their nosey tips,
And beat a drum,
And catch a bar,
And wiggle with
How pleased they are.

DOROTHY ALDIS

49

The Talking Tiger

If a tiger
Walks beside you
And he whispers:
"Where are you going?"
Do not answer,
Just keep walking
Just keep walking, walking, walking.
And if he continues talking
You keep walking.
Let him talk.

You just walk.
A talking tiger
Never bites,
A walking tiger
Never fights.
But if you find
That he's a bore
Then go right home
And shut the door.

ARNOLD SPILKA

51

Lost in the Zoo

If I were lost
    Inside the zoo,
I think that this
    Is what I'd do.

I'd say, "Giraffe,
    Please look around —
Your head is high
    Above the ground —

Will you point out
    To me, the place
Where you can see
    My mother's face?"

ILO ORLEANS

52

The Camel

The camel has a single hump;
The dromedary, two;
Or else the other way around.
I'm never sure. Are you?

OGDEN NASH

53

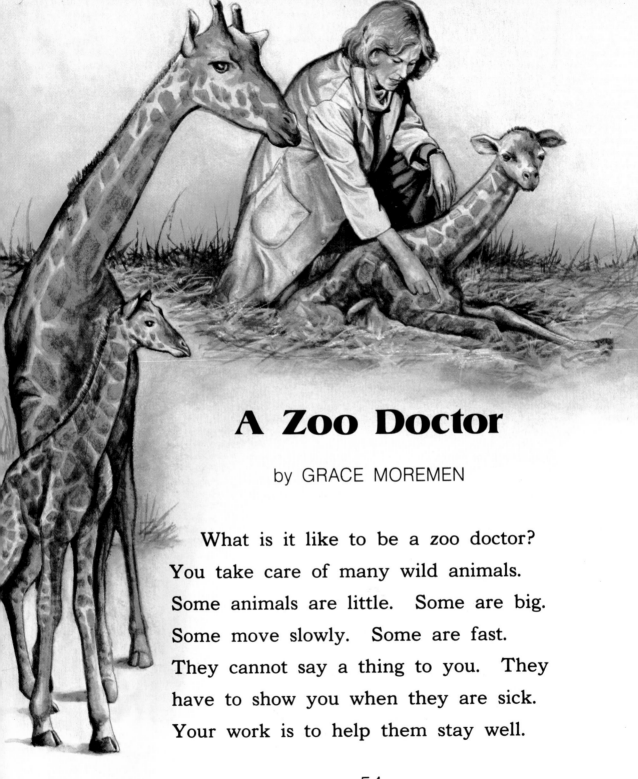

A Zoo Doctor

by GRACE MOREMEN

What is it like to be a zoo doctor?
You take care of many wild animals.
Some animals are little.   Some are big.
Some move slowly.   Some are fast.
They cannot say a thing to you.   They
have to show you when they are sick.
Your work is to help them stay well.

Let's go with a zoo doctor. Let's work for a day. Then we will know what a zoo doctor's work is.

It is morning. The doctor sees the sickest animals first. They are in the zoo hospital.

Today the doctor looks at a little fox. This fox fell. It cannot walk. The doctor works on the fox's leg. Soon the fox will walk and run once more.

Next the doctor goes outside. The first stop is at the monkey house. One monkey is not playing. It is not eating at all.

The doctor looks at the monkey. It looks scared. The doctor tells the helper to take it to the zoo hospital. The monkey will get well in the hospital.

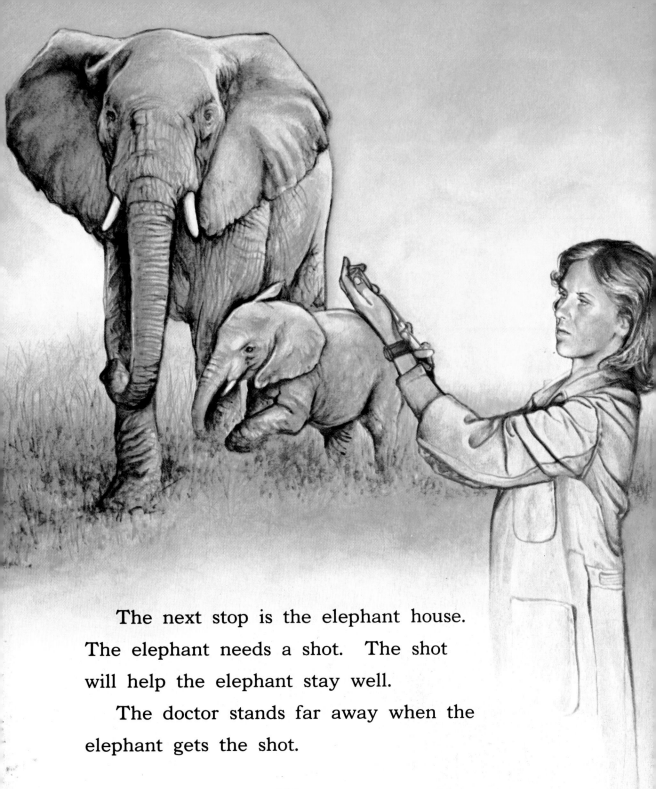

The next stop is the elephant house.
The elephant needs a shot. The shot
will help the elephant stay well.

The doctor stands far away when the
elephant gets the shot.

Morning is over. The doctor stops to see a mother lion. She has two little lions. They are the newest animals in the zoo. The doctor is happy. The little lions are doing very well.

It is afternoon. The doctor goes back
to the hospital to look at some birds that
have just come to the zoo.

The doctor looks them over with great
care. "They are fine," the doctor says.

The helper takes the birds outside to
the cage. Now all the people can come
see the bright, beautiful birds.

Then the doctor looks at some pictures. The pictures show a bigger home for the bears. Will the bears be happy in the new home? Do they have room to play? Does the home have room for more bears? The doctor thinks and makes some notes.

The doctor's day is over. It is time to go home. The doctor has worked to take care of the animals.

You have spent a day with the zoo
doctor. Now you know what a zoo doctor
does. The doctor works to make the zoo
animals happy and well.

Ling-Ling and Hsing-Hsing

Some stories are made up of facts. Facts tell about things. Facts tell you who, what, when, where, why, or how. Facts are true.

Here are some facts about Ling-Ling and Hsing-Hsing.

Ling-Ling and Hsing-Hsing are two pandas from China. In 1972, they moved to a zoo in America. Ling-Ling and Hsing-Hsing are the first pandas to live in America since 1953.

A story can be fiction. Fiction is a story that a writer makes up. Some fiction has facts in it. Other fiction does not.

Read this story that a writer made up about Ling-Ling and Hsing-Hsing.

Jim liked pandas. One day he heard that Ling-Ling and Hsing-Hsing were moving to the city zoo. Jim met the pandas when they came to their new home. He called to them, "I am glad that you have come to our zoo."

Tell three things that went on in the story.

Find out which of the stories are fact and which are fiction. Ask, "Does it tell me true things, or does it tell me a story?" Then tell if the story is fact or fiction.

1. Pam went to see Ling-Ling and Hsing-Hsing. When Hsing-Hsing saw Pam, he rolled over. Pam laughed and said, "Roll over again, Hsing-Hsing!"

2. Zookeepers tell people about the pandas. But that is only part of their job. Zookeepers must take care of all the animals. They make sure that all the animals are happy and well.

3. Pandas do not live together in the woods of China. Each panda lives away from the others. That is why Ling-Ling and Hsing-Hsing have their own cages at the zoo.

Tools

TOOLS FOR WORK

What are tools? Tools are things we use when we do work. The right tools help us do better work.

Three people are working outside. They are using tools. What tools do they have? How do tools help them?

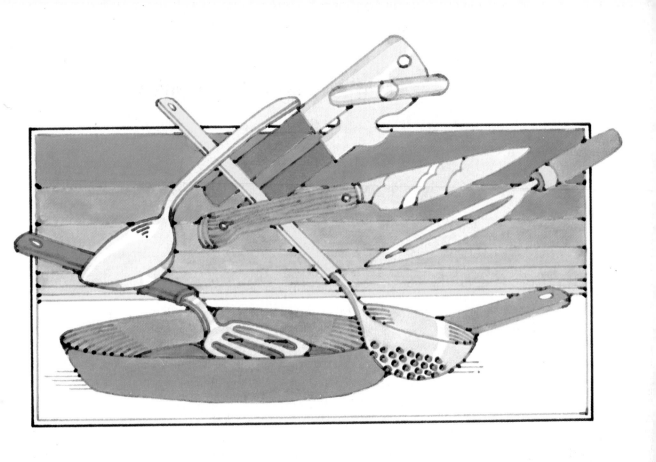

We use tools inside, too. Spoons are
tools. They are used for many things.
What is the fastest way to get an egg
up out of hot water? Can you think of
other uses for spoons?

Name some tools people use when
they make lunch. What do they use to
peel potatoes? What do they use to cut
up the food?

Many people use tools when they work away from home. The pictures show some of the tools.

What tool is the man using? Why?

What tools are the workers using to make a deep hole?

What tool is the woman using?

Boys and girls work, too. They work at home and at school. So they need tools. Here are some tools used in school. Can you name them?

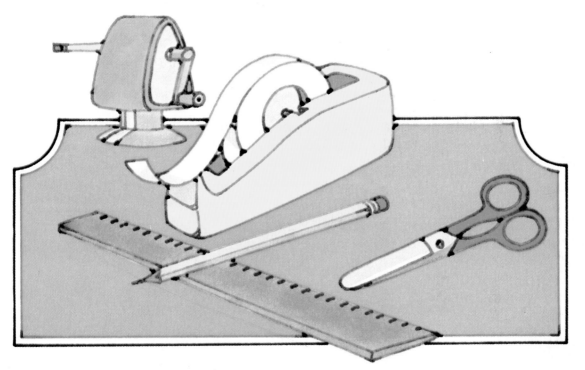

You know them very well. You have used them many times in your work.

Tools are useful things to have. Good tools help us do good work, at home, outside, and at school.

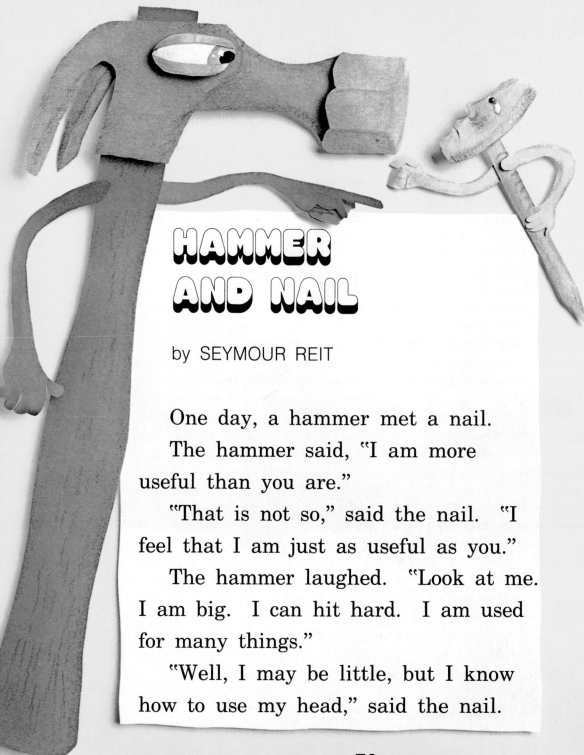

HAMMER AND NAIL

by SEYMOUR REIT

One day, a hammer met a nail.
The hammer said, "I am more useful than you are."

"That is not so," said the nail. "I feel that I am just as useful as you."

The hammer laughed. "Look at me. I am big. I can hit hard. I am used for many things."

"Well, I may be little, but I know how to use my head," said the nail.

"That may be," said the hammer. "But still, I am more useful than you."

The nail was quiet after that.

A woman came into the room. She picked up the hammer and the nail. She put the nail up. She hit it on the head with the hammer. She hit it again and again. Soon the nail was deep in the wall.

The woman put the hammer down. She picked up a picture. She put the picture on the nail. Then she went out of the room.

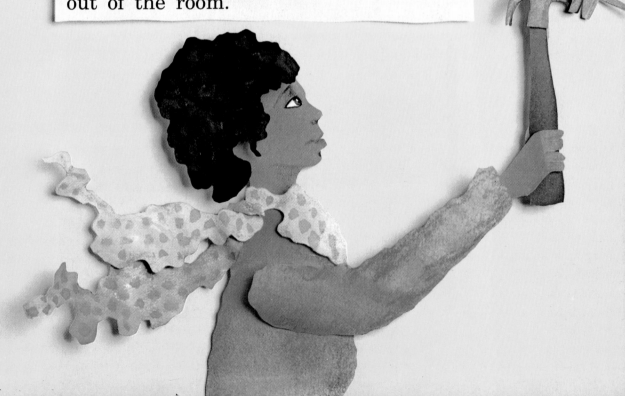

The nail laughed. "Now you see, Hammer? I am useful, too. I can make a picture stay up."

The hammer laughed, too. Then it said, "You are right, Little Nail. I am useful. And you are useful. But we are the most useful of all when we work together!"

TOOLS

Paint a picture.
Cut down wheat.
Peel potatoes.
Clean the street.

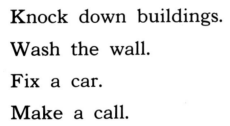

Knock down buildings.
Wash the wall.
Fix a car.
Make a call.

Plant some carrots.
Build three schools.
What do we use?
Tools, tools, tools!

73

Then and Now

by SEYMOUR REIT

Some of the first tools were rocks.
Long ago, people used rocks as hammers.
They used rocks to cut things. The
rock tools were hard to use.

Time went by. People made tools
that were better.

People needed wood for houses.
They made saws. With saws they cut
down big trees. The trees were cut
into logs. Then they sawed the logs
into the wood they needed.

We still use saws today. But
today's saw mills can cut up many
logs very fast.

People needed to move things. At first, things were moved on the backs of people. Then people used teams of animals. After a time, people made wagons for the animals to pull. But moving things by wagon was hard work.

Today we have cars, trains, boats, and planes. With them, it is easy to move things many miles across land and sea.

Once, most of the land was wild. People wanted to build houses and streets on it. They wanted to grow things on the land. But first they had to move the rocks and trees away.

They did that, using teams of animals. It was slow work, and it was not easy.

That is not so today. Today we have bulldozers. Bulldozers work fast. They are better than teams of animals.

As time went by, people made more and more tools to do more and more things. Today we have many tools. Some tools help sick people. Some of the tools help us grow food and bake bread. Some help us build things. Some help us move things. And some help us fly to the moon!

Pencils

Children use many tools in school. One tool is a pencil.

Some people think that pencils have lead in them. But did you know that pencils have no real lead at all?

Real lead is soft. It is dark gray.
But what you see in pencils is not
really lead. It just looks like lead, so
it is called lead.

The "lead" in pencils is made from
graphite. People dig up graphite from
the land. Graphite, together with clay
and water, is used to make the lead
for pencils.

How are pencils made? Many things are needed. First of all, a piece of wood is needed.

Cuts are made in the wood. Then pencil leads are put in the cuts. How many pencils can be made from this piece of wood?

A piece of wood is put on top of the first piece. The two pieces of wood are put together.

Then the wood is cut. The pieces can make three pencils.

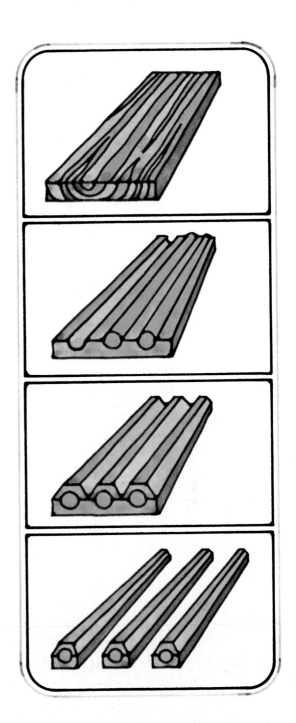

Next, the pencil is painted. An eraser is put on. A band is put around the eraser. That helps the eraser stay on the pencil.

After that the pencils go into boxes. They are quickly sent to people all over the world.

As you use a pencil, the leads gets small. What tool is used to cut the wood away?

As time goes by, the pencil gets small, too. You cannot do neat work with it. What do you do then? Yes, you get a new pencil. And you go back to work!

What Am I?

Look and see if you can find me in the picture.

When you want to fix something on a paper, I am a useful friend. What am I?

To use me, you have to hit me again and again. What am I?

If you are an egg, I can get you out of hot water. What am I?

I have many teeth. But I do not eat. What am I?

83

CRAYONS

You do many things in school. What
do you like to do best? Many children
like to color. What do you use when you
color? Yes, you use crayons.

How are crayons made? First, people
get a big piece of wax. The wax is
heated until it is soft.

Colors are put into the soft wax.
Blue coloring is used for blue crayons,
red coloring for red crayons, and so on.

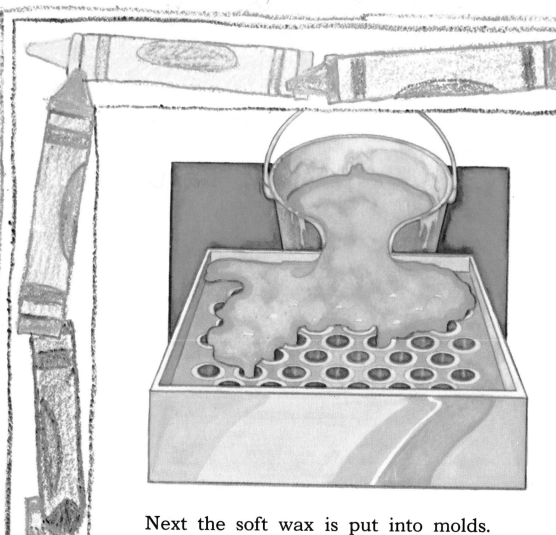

Next the soft wax is put into molds. The wax gets cold in the molds. It gets hard. The hard pieces of colored wax are crayons.

Paper is put around the crayons. Then the newly made crayons are put into boxes. They are sent to you.

Do you have any crayons at school? What color do you use up first? Is it the color you like best?

Crayons are lots of fun to use. But remember one thing. Keep any crayons you have away from too much heat.

Why?

This is why!

A New Kind of Picture

This girl is making a new kind of picture. It is called a rubbing.

You can make a rubbing. Just put something under a piece of paper. Then rub the paper with a pencil.

Can you tell what this girl put under her paper?

You can use colored pencils or crayons to make rubbings, too. Peel the paper from the crayon first. Here are some pictures that you can make.

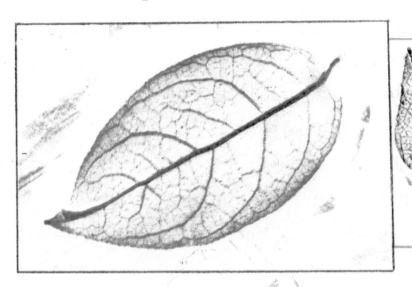

Rubbings of Leaves

Put some leaves on a sheet of paper. Put a new sheet of paper over the leaves. Rub over the top sheet with colored pencils or crayons.

Show the leaves' summer color with green. Show the leaves' fall colors with red and yellow.

Rubbings of People

Cut a sheet of paper to look like a friend's head.

Cut pieces of paper for the eyes, ears, and so on. Put them on the cutout of the head.

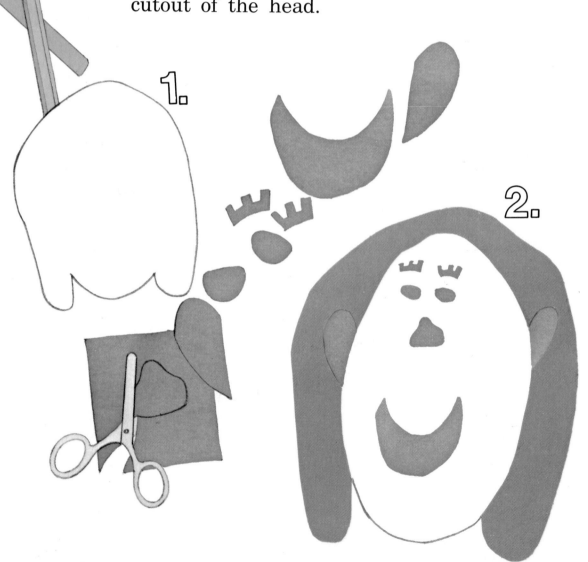

Put the cutout on a sheet of paper.
Put a sheet of paper over the cutout.
Make a rubbing.

Then move the cutout under your
top sheet. Make many rubbings of
your friend.

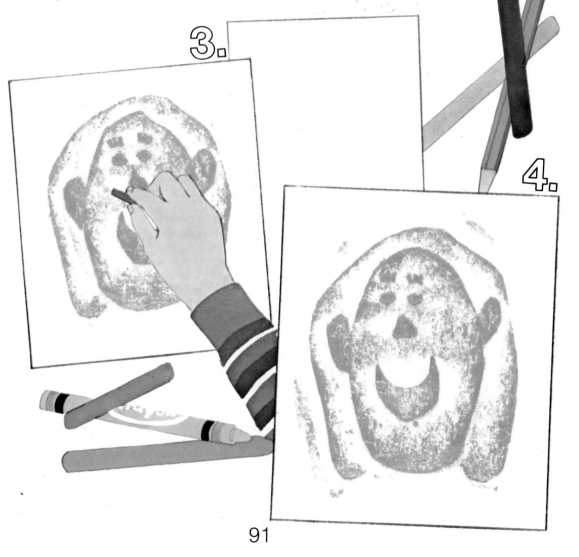

Trees in the Woods

Woods Rubbing

Make cutouts of three kinds of trees. Then use the cutouts over and over. Use green, red, yellow, and brown pencils or crayons. Make lots of trees. The rubbing can be named "Trees in the Woods."

City Rubbing

You can make a rubbing of a city, too. Cut out big buildings. Cut out a car and bus. Cut out some people and trees.

Then take out your colors. Make many rubbings. This picture can be very, very big!

Words As Tools

Did you know that words can be tools? Titles and subtitles are tools for finding out things.

Titles can be the names of parts of books. Subtitles can be the names of smaller parts. We use titles and subtitles to find out where things are in books.

Find the titles and subtitles in this book about tools.

1. "Tools From Long Ago" is the first title. Are the two lines under it called subtitles or titles?

2. How many subtitles are there in the book? Read them.

3. Where might you look to find out about bulldozers?

4. What title and subtitles help you find out about the first tools made by people?

5. Look at the picture. What title might tell about these tools?

6. Make up a new subtitle for the tools you see in the picture.

Some newspaper ads have titles and subtitles, too. Read this one.

Try This

Look at the things below. Tell what floor and what shop would have each thing.

1. a hat for Dad
2. a rocking chair
3. an ant farm
4. a potato peeler
5. a toy ball
6. shoes for Mom

96

Animals at Play

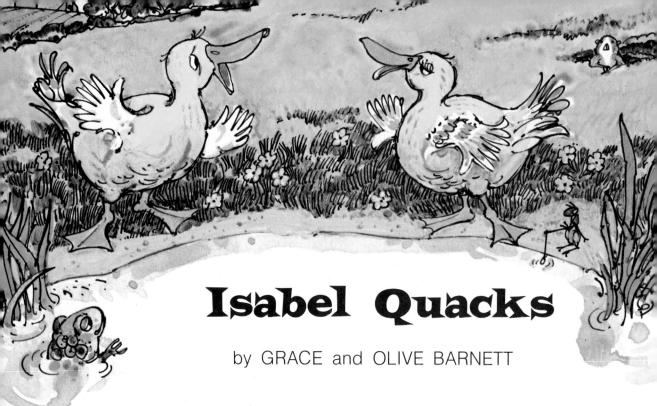

Isabel Quacks

by GRACE and OLIVE BARNETT

Isabel was a bright duck. She swam and floated as well as all ducks do. She walked as well as they do, too.

But Isabel did not do one thing. She did not quack!

One day her mother said, "Why not try to quack, Isabel? All the other ducks on the farm quack."

Isabel said, "I can quack if I want to. I do not need to quack. So I do not do it."

But Isabel's mother was not so sure.
She had never heard Isabel quack, not
one time. Did Isabel really know how
to quack? Only Isabel knew for sure.

One day, Isabel was out walking.
She saw a big green grasshopper. Isabel
jumped for it. But she was too slow.
The grasshopper got away.

As Isabel jumped, a piece of rope
got around her leg. She pulled and
pulled. But that only made the rope
cut into her leg.

A white cat came by. "Hello, Isabel," he said. "You need help. Say meow. That is what I say when I need help."

Isabel said, "Cats' meows are fine for cats. But it is not what a duck says. When a duck needs help, she quacks."

The cat smiled. "We all know that you cannot quack, Isabel," he said. "You had better say meow."

Just then, a brown dog came up. He said, "Isabel, go bow-wow. Then the girl will come and help you."

Isabel said, "Dogs' bow-wows are fine for dogs. But they are all wrong for ducks. Ducks go quack."

The dog laughed. "Ducks can quack. But you cannot quack, Isabel. You had better say bow-wow."

Well, one by one, the animals came up to Isabel. One by one, they told her what sound to make. Each time, Isabel said, "No, that is wrong. I will quack."

And each time, the animals said, "We know that you cannot quack, Isabel."

At last all the animals were in a row around Isabel. The rooster said, "If you are going to quack, you must do it soon."

Isabel said, "I will. Stand back."

The animals did that. They waited. Then Isabel quacked.

"Quack. QUACK! **QUACK!!**"

They were great quacks. They were the best quacks of all!

At once a girl who lived on the farm ran out of the house. She raced up to Isabel.

"Do you need help, Isabel?" she asked. And she helped Isabel to get rid of the rope.

Then the girl went back inside.

The rooster said, "That was some quacking, Isabel. That was really some quacking!"

After that, Isabel swam and floated like a duck. She walked like a duck. And she quacked like a duck. But she did not quack much. She only quacked when she needed to.

The Birthday Party

by DINA ANASTASIO

The animals in the play are:

Bear

Clam

Bee

Cat

Rabbit

Mouse

Dog

Fox

(Cat, Rabbit, and Bear are together.)

CAT: My friends, we must get to
   work. Tomorrow is Elephant's
   birthday, and we must throw a
   surprise birthday party for her.

RABBIT: We have so many things to
   do. How can we do it all?

BEAR: I know. We will ask each
   friend to do one thing.

CAT: Who will we ask to get the cake?

RABBIT: How about Dog? You know what they say. "Dog is man's best friend." So Dog can ask his best friend to make the cake.

BEAR: That is fine. Now, who will we get to think up some games?

CAT: I know. We will get Bee.

RABBIT: No, no, not Bee. Bee is too busy. You know what they say. "Busy as a bee."

BEAR: I know. How about Mouse?
That is a good, quiet thing for a
mouse to do. You know what they
say. "Quiet as a mouse."

CAT: Yes, good. Now, what about
jokes? Who will tell the jokes?

RABBIT: I am sure that Clam can do
it. You know, "Happy as a clam."

BEAR: Good, and Fox can get Elephant
to the party. "Sly as a fox" and all
that. Old Fox will not tell the
surprise to Elephant.

(It is the next day. Cat, Rabbit, and Bear are together. Dog comes in.)

CAT: Oh, good, here is Dog. But where is the cake?

DOG: Well, when I asked my best friend to make a cake, he was not very polite. He just laughed at me. Man's best friend, ho!

RABBIT: Oh, no, what will we do? We have no cake.

(Mouse comes in.)

BEAR: Well, here is Mouse. I am sure that you have some games.

MOUSE: Oh, no, I do not! My brothers were playing and screaming all day long. So I didn't think up one game for the party.

CAT: Oh, no! No cake, no games. This is going to be some party.

RABBIT: Well, here comes Clam. He
will make us happy with his jokes.

CLAM: Oh me, oh my. I am so sad.
Soon winter will come. Then I'll be
cold. Oh, me!

BEAR: But Clam, where are the jokes?

CLAM: Jokes? Ho! That is a joke. I
am so sad. Who can think of jokes
at a time like this?

(<u>Fox runs in.</u>)

FOX: Well, how is it going?

CAT: Where is Elephant?

FOX: She will be here soon. I told her that we were having a surprise party for her, so she will be here.

RABBIT: You **told** her? And they say that you are sly? Oh me, this is going to be some party.

(<u>Bee walks in slowly.</u>)

BEE: Well, here I am. I did not have a thing to do. So I came by to have some food and fun. Say, is this party for Elephant?

CAT: It is. Why?

BEE: I just saw her. She said she was
about to go to sleep. So I said,
"What about your party?"

RABBIT: And what did she say?

BEE: She said, "What party?"

BEAR: Oh, she did not remember.

ALL: But how can that be? Elephants
never forget!

Timothy Turtle

by ALICE VAUGHT DAVIS

Timothy Turtle lived in the woods next to a river. He was a very old turtle. He had lived by the river for many years. All the animals that lived in the woods liked him.

But his very best friend was Frog. She lived by a tree next to the river.

Timothy liked to take Frog on his back for a ride up the river.

Timothy liked to swim in the water. He liked to sit by the river and sleep in the sun.

But best of all he liked to slide down a hill. The hill was in the woods not far from the river.

One morning Timothy went for a slide. The hill was wet from a rain that had come in the night. He went very fast. On his way down the hill, he rolled over on his back.

Now Timothy's shell was very big. Hard as he tried, he did not turn himself over. He stayed on his back, kicking his legs in the air. He kicked and kicked and kicked. He tried very hard. But he did not turn his big shell over.

Squirrel, who lived in the tree by the river, saw Timothy. He came to ask what was wrong.

"What is your problem, Timothy?" asked Squirrel.

"I fell on my back and cannot turn over. Can you help me?" asked Timothy.

But Squirrel was too little to help.

"I will go and find help," said
Squirrel. So he ran into the woods and
met Rabbit.

"Come quickly," said Squirrel.
"Timothy Turtle fell on his back and
cannot turn over."

They ran back to Timothy. Squirrel
and Rabbit pushed. But they did not
turn him over.

"I will go and find more help," said
Squirrel. He ran into the woods until
he saw Possum sleeping in the sun.

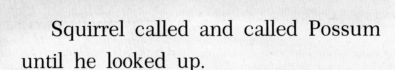

Squirrel called and called Possum until he looked up.

"Come quickly," said Squirrel. "Timothy Turtle has a problem. He fell on his back and cannot turn over."

"I'll see what I can do," said Possum slowly. He got up and walked slowly after Squirrel.

"Will you walk a little faster, Mr. Possum?"

"I will," said Possum. He walked as fast as a possum can walk. So on they went until they came to Timothy.

But Squirrel and Rabbit and Possum did not turn Timothy over.

They sat looking at Timothy and thinking about what to do. Timothy was still kicking his legs in the air and trying to turn himself over.

Now Frog had heard them. She came to see what was going on. She sat on the hill and laughed. She laughed so loud that the animals all turned and looked at her.

"What are you laughing about?" asked Squirrel.

"I am laughing at all of you," said Frog.

"If you think it is so funny, tell us how we can turn Timothy over."

"I will," said Frog. "Just take him by the shell. Push him down to the river. When he falls in the water, he will turn over."

So Squirrel pushed on Timothy's shell. Possum pushed on Squirrel. Rabbit pushed on Possum. They pushed and pushed until they got Timothy down to the river.

Splash! went the water. Timothy fell in and turned over.

Timothy swam in the water until he had washed his shell. Then he came out of the river. He thanked his friends for helping him.

Rabbit and Possum and Squirrel sat on the hill. They laughed as Timothy Turtle gave Frog a ride up the river on his back.

The Elephant on the Bus

by RUBE ROSEN

The blue bus stopped at the bus stop. A man got off and an elephant got on. The bus driver looked at the elephant.

He said, "Oh, no, you cannot ride on my bus."

The elephant said, "But I must get back to the zoo. It is time for supper."

"But you still cannot ride on my bus," the driver said. "You are much too big!"

The elephant was unhappy. He said, "I am pretty small for an elephant. I will not take up very much room."

The people on the bus asked the driver to let the elephant come onto the bus.

The bus driver looked unhappy. Then he said, "All right. You can ride on my bus. But you may not use more than one seat."

So the elephant got inside the bus. He sat down. He pulled his feet in and rolled up his trunk. He sat very still in the seat.

At the next stop, a woman got on. She sat in the seat in front of the elephant. She had on a pretty red hat with a long feather. The feather went back over the seat. It tickled the elephant's trunk.

The bus went on. The feather went
up and down. And this tickled the
elephant's trunk more. The elephant
felt as if he were going to sneeze.

The elephant wanted to move. But
a man was sitting next to him. He
wanted to ask the woman to take off
her hat. But his trunk was rolled up.
So he did not say a thing.

The feather went up and down, up
and down. It tickled him more and
more.

The elephant swelled up.

He felt . . . oh . . . oh. . . .

He felt . . . he felt . . . oh . . . oh.

AH . . . CHOOO!

It was a **big** sneeze!

The elephant's trunk unrolled. He
sneezed all the hats in the bus right
up into the air.

The red hat with the big feather landed on the driver's head. The driver's hat landed on the elephant's head. A big man's hat landed on a little girl's head. Each hat landed on other people's heads. The people and the elephant looked very silly.

The driver stopped the bus. All the people got the right hats back. Then the driver said the elephant had to get off the bus. All the people said it was the best thing to do, too.

So the elephant got off the bus. He walked back to the zoo. On the way he had one more big sneeze. But he was outside. So no one's hat came off.

And from that day on, you never see an elephant on a bus.

It Is Raining—Cats and Dogs

Sometimes people say, "It is raining cats and dogs!" Does that mean that cats and dogs are falling from the sky? No, it does not. What does it really mean?

Here are some stories. Can you tell what the underlined words really mean?

Kim was busy. She cut the grass. She helped her father clean the windows. Then she went in to clean up her room.

"Wait, Kim," said her father. "You helped me. Now I'll give you a hand with your room."

"Come quickly, Carla," called Linda. "The school bus is here."

"Yes, come on," said Tom. "We are going to be late for school."

"Hold your horses," said Carla. "I'm putting on my shoes."

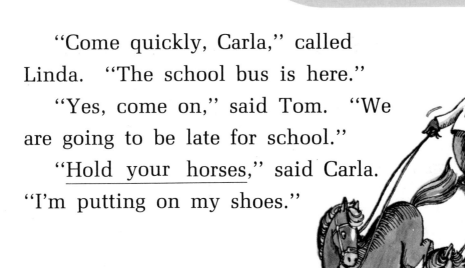

"I am going to your birthday party, Maria," said Jack.

"What birthday party?" said Maria.

"Is it a surprise party?" asked Jack.

"I just let the cat out of the bag."

Try This

What do the underlined words mean?

1. Jill has no time to play today. She wants to clean the house before night. She is as busy as a bee. Jill is flying from flower to flower.
is working hard all day long.

2. One day Maria got wet in the rain. Her mother said, "Put on these dry things and sit by the fire. I'll make you a hot drink. Soon you will be as snug as a bug in a rug." Maria will feel like a bug.
will be warm and happy.

128

By the Sea

(To be read by the teacher.)

Upon the Beach

Upon the beach
With pail and spade,
My sandy pies and wells I made.

And people passed
On every hand
And left their footprints on the sand.

Then came a wave
With the rushing tide —
And everything was washed aside.

ILO ORLEANS

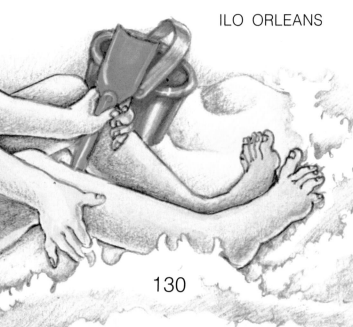

The Wave

by DINA ANASTASIO

It was a good hot day. Many people were at the beach. Carla saw them. They were jumping and laughing in the water. They were waiting for the waves.

Carla was not doing that. Carla had not been in the water all afternoon. She was scared of the water.

Until this morning, Carla had loved the water. She liked to jump and ride the waves more than her friends did.

But this morning something had happened. Now she did not want to go near the water.

What had happened to scare Carla so? Carla remembered. This morning she had been in the water near the beach. She was waiting for the waves to come. Then a giant wave came.

That wave hit Carla and pulled her under. It turned her over and over. Carla started to get up. But the giant wave pulled her down again. Carla was so scared that she stopped thinking.

Then a woman saw what was happening. She pulled Carla out of the water. That was it. That was all.

Carla was all right now. But she did not forget how it had felt under that giant wave.

Carla started to read her book again. But it was no use. She looked out at her friends. They were splashing and playing in the big waves.

Nearby, Carla's little brother, Ted, was jumping the waves that rolled up to the beach. Then, as Carla looked on, a wave hit Ted. It pulled him under.

Carla waited for him to come up. But Ted stayed under. No one but Carla saw that Ted needed help.

Carla jumped up and ran to the water. She tried to get to her brother. But as she did, a wave pulled her under, too. She was more scared than this morning! Then she saw Ted's scared look. Carla knew that she had no time to be scared. She had to help. She got to Ted and pulled him out of the wave. She helped him back up to the beach.

Ted was all right. But he was scared.
"I'll never go in the water again!" he said.

Carla looked at her brother. She
remembered the day. All day Carla had
sat on the beach. All day she had
stayed away from the fun of the water.

Carla felt very uneasy. But she said, "Come on, Ted. I'll go in with you."

"All right," said Ted. He put his hand in Carla's hand. They went down to the water.

Then, going very slowly, they walked together, hand in hand, out into the waves.

What the Sea Has a Lot Of

Oh, I went down to the sea,
   I did,
I went to the sea to get
A little thing—a circus ring—
And all I got was wet.

Then I went back to the sea,
   I did,
I went back down to get
A little cat in a feathered hat—
You know what I got? Wet.

So I tried it one more time,
    I did,
I went once more to get
A red and blue city zoo—
What did I get? Yes. Wet.

Oh, the sea, it has no shoes,
    Oh no,
It has no TV set.
But the sea has got
A great big lot,
A really big lot of wet!

Tuffy the Dolphin

This is about a dolphin that worked with people. It happened in 1965. The people were trying to find out about the sea. They started by building a house in the sea. The house was called "Sealab II." And they lived for a time in that house under the water!

The dolphin's name was Tuffy. He helped the people in many ways. People put tools on Tuffy's back. He swam with the tools to people who were waiting outside Sealab II.

But most of all, Tuffy the dolphin was a friend. Tuffy was trained to help people if they got lost under the water. Here is how the people trained Tuffy to do that.

It was a fall day in 1965. The sea was very still. But under the sea, the people of Sealab II were busy training Tuffy. One of the people swam down into the dark water. He looked for a cave to hide in. At last, he saw one.

The man swam into the cave.
Then he turned a tool on. The tool
made a sound that Tuffy could hear
from far away. Could Tuffy use the
sound to find the man? Could Tuffy
help the man return to Sealab II?
The man did not know. So he sat in
the cave in the sea and waited.

Tuffy was swimming up and down outside Sealab II. He knew that his friend was hiding under the sea. He waited for the sound.

At last, Tuffy heard it. He started to go after the sound. But as he swam down, the sound got softer. Then Tuffy could not hear it at all.

Tuffy knew that his friend was near. But he could not find him! Tuffy did not know what to do.

Tuffy was about to return to Sealab
II. Then he heard the sound again.
It was very soft. But it was all Tuffy
needed. Quickly he swam to the cave
where the man was hiding. He saw
his friend!

But the man stayed still. He wanted
to see if Tuffy could help him move.
Tuffy could. Slowly, Tuffy pulled the
man out of the cave.

The man and the dolphin were soon home again. That made the people of Sealab II very happy. Tuffy had used the sound to find the man. He had removed him from the cave. He had returned the man to Sealab II.

Now the people felt better about working under the sea. If one of them got lost, the friendly dolphin, Tuffy, could soon find him!

(To be read by the teacher.)

Sea Calm

How still,
How strangely still
The water is today.
It is not good
For water
To be so still that way.

LANGSTON HUGHES

(To be read by the teacher.)

Haiku

We rowed into fog . . .
and out through fog. . . . Oh how blue,
how bright the wide sea!

SHIKI

147

Who Says a Fish Can't Talk?

by DINA ANASTASIO

For this play you will need people to play:

Carla   Bobby   Isabel   Timothy

Big Log   Big Fish   Storyteller

And you will need:

4 fishing lines   4 chairs

STORYTELLER: This is a story about a boy who was named Timothy, a girl named Isabel, a boy named Bobby, and a girl named Carla.

(As the names are called, Timothy, Isabel, Bobby, and Carla come in. They bow.)

STORYTELLER: One day the four friends went fishing together by the sea.

(The friends stand in a line. Then Timothy walks out to the front. He throws out his fishing line.)

TIMOTHY: My, what a great day for fishing! I'll pull in lots of fish today. Wait, I think I feel something. It's a giant one! I'll pull it in.

(Big Fish jumps up and down.)

BIG FISH: Let me go! Let me go!

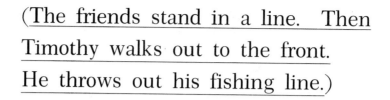

(Timothy throws down his line and runs over to Isabel.)

TIMOTHY: It talked, Isabel, it talked! I just caught a great big fish and it talked!

ISABEL: Now that's silly, Timothy. You know that fish can't talk. Go away and let me fish.

TIMOTHY: No more fishing for me today. I am going to sit on that big log and think this over.

(Timothy sits in the first chair.)

ISABEL: Oh, my! I think that I have caught a big one!

BIG FISH: Let me go! Let me go!

(Isabel runs to Bobby.)

ISABEL: Bobby! Listen, Bobby! I just caught a talking fish!

BOBBY: How silly can you get? Fish can't talk. Please go away and let me fish.

(Isabel sits down next to Timothy.)

BOBBY: Oh, boy, just look at that fish! That's what I call a big fish!

BIG FISH: Let me go! Let me go!

(Bobby runs over to Carla.)

BOBBY: Listen to me, Carla! I have just caught a talking fish!

CARLA: Oh, come on, now. Fish don't talk. Kindly go away and let me fish!

(Bobby sits down next to Isabel.)

CARLA: I think I got something. Yes, I did! It's a big fish. I'll just pull it in slowly.

BIG FISH: Let me go! Let me go!

(Carla runs over to the others.)

CARLA: You were right, that big fish can talk!

TIMOTHY: This is so silly!

ISABEL: I'll say it's silly!

BOBBY: I'll say it's silly!

CARLA: I'll say it's silly!

BIG LOG: Really? What's so silly about a
   talking fish? I don't think it's silly at all!
ALL: The log! It's talking!

(They jump up and run off, screaming.)

STORYTELLER: And that's the story of the fish
   that talked. Say good-by, my friends.
BIG FISH and BIG LOG: Good-by, my friends.

(The three bow and walk off.)

By the Beautiful Sea

By the sea, by the sea
By the beautiful sea—
You and I, you and I
Oh! how happy we'll be—

When each wave comes a-rolling in
We will duck or swim
And we'll float and fool around the water

Over and under
And then up for air—
Dad is rich, Mom is rich,
So now what do we care?

I love to be beside your side,
beside the sea,
beside the seaside
By the beautiful sea.

Can You Read the Whole Thing?

<u>Seen</u> is a new word. How can you read words that you have never <u>seen</u> before? This is what to do.

1. You use what you know about words. The word <u>seen</u> starts like <u>see</u> and ends like <u>green</u>.

2. You read the other words in the sentence and think about them. They can help you work out the meaning of the new word. Did the other words help you to see that <u>seen</u> means the same as <u>looked at</u>?

This story has some words that you may not know. See if you can read the whole thing.

Do you know how we get water? First rain falls from the clouds. Then the water runs into rivers, or <u>streams</u>.

158

Some of the water in the streams flows into the sea.

The air over the sea is wet air. It holds some of the water from the sea below. The sun heats up the sea and the air. The sun's heat makes the wet air go up, or rise, into the clouds. There the air cools down. Then the rain starts all over again.

Can you find a new word in the story that . . .

- has the vowel sound of know?
- means go up?
- is the opposite of makes hot?
- has the vowel sound of feet?
- means runs off into?
- has the vowel sound of mine?
- means under it?
- has the vowel sound of tool?
- means rivers?

1. The fishing fleet went out to sea.
   A fishing <u>fleet</u> is made up of

   _____ .

       old trains   funny ducks
           fishing boats

2. You can see the lighthouse
   glowing in the dark.
   Something that <u>glows</u> _____ .

     shines   breaks   makes noise

3. Dolphins can move with great
   speed in the water.
   Something that has <u>speed</u> is

   _____ .

         old   fast   dark

4. The toad jumped from its home
   in the pond to the land.
   A <u>toad</u> is an animal like a _____ .

         cat   frog   dog

Americans All

Jim Beckwourth, Mountain Man

His name was Jim Beckwourth. He lived long ago, when America was still young. He was a mountain man. What did mountain men do? They hunted for wild animals in the mountains of the West.

The Long Walk

When Jim was a young man, he went on a hunt with many other men. The men went on horses. One night, all their horses ran away.

Jim and a man named Harris were
sent to get some new horses. They
would have to walk for many days.

Now Harris was sure that he was a
very fast walker. He laughed, "You
are too slow, Jim. You will not keep
up with me."

Jim laughed. "Walk your fastest,"
he said. "We will see who stops first."

Harris walked fast and far the first
day. So did Jim. Night fell, and
Harris wanted to stop.

"So soon?" asked Jim. "Why, I was
just getting started."

The men had to hunt for food as they went along. One day, they found no game at all. The next day came. Again, they found no food to eat. Many days passed. The hungry men walked on. But they went more and more slowly.

Jim knew that they must keep walking. If they did not, they would die in the wilds.

One day, Harris stopped. He sat on the ground. "I can walk no more," he said sadly.

Jim said, "Stay here. I'll get help."

All that day, Jim walked and walked. At last he could not go on. He fell to the ground.

Just then, he saw some Indians. Jim shouted to them. He and Harris were saved!

The Indians took the men to their home and gave them food. In no time at all, Jim and Harris were well once more, thanks to the kind Indians.

Jim said, "Well, we did not get the horses, Harris. But now you know who the better walker is!"

The Bears

One time, Jim was out hunting with
a friend. All at once, a big bear ran at
them. Jim jumped to one side and ran.

But his friend was not so fast. The
bear got him. Fast as lightning, Jim
turned and shot the bear.

No sooner was the bear down than
a new bear ran at the man. This bear
was bigger than the first!

Jim was far away. Could he get
the bear? Would he hit his friend?
He fired. The bear fell.

Jim had saved his friend two times
that morning.

The Crow Indians

Mountain men like to tell a kind of story. This kind of story is called a tall tale. One morning, some Crow Indians were talking to a friend of Jim's. The friend told them a tall tale. He said that Jim was a Crow Indian, too. He said that Jim had been lost by the Indians many years ago, when the Crow were fighting with other Indians. Jim laughed to himself. He went along with the tale.

But the Crow did not laugh. They took Jim back with them to their home. They gave him Indian clothes to put on. They soon found out about the tall tale. But they liked Jim. They called him brother.

167

Jim lived with the Crow for many
years. As time went by, he came to
love his Indian friends and their ways.
The Crow felt that Jim was a fine
hunter and a wise man.

After a time, Jim was made one of
the chiefs of the Crow Indians. He
worked hard to be a good, wise chief.

Beckwourth Pass

After many years, Jim left the Crow. He crossed the mountains to the West. He lived in the new land where people had found gold.

Jim did not find gold. But he did find an easy way to get across the tall mountains. He helped other people to use the pass he had found. Today that pass is called "Beckwourth Pass."

Today many people know about Jim Beckwourth. They know that he was one of the greatest mountain men.

Betty Zane

The British Horses

This happened a long time ago, when Americans were fighting to be free from the British.

Betty Zane lived in an American city. One night, many British soldiers stopped in front of her father's house. One of the soldiers came in. He said, "Master Zane, I want food for my men."

Betty's father did not want to give
the food, but he had to do it. All the
soldiers came into the house.

Betty ran up to her room and looked
out the window. She could see many
British horses outside. Betty knew that
the American soldiers needed horses.
What could she do?

She saw that all the horses were
roped together. She made up a plan.

Quietly, Betty went out of the house. She ran down the walk and got up on the first horse. Slowly, she took the long line of horses down the dark street.

Betty took the horses away to the Americans. Then she ran home and went inside. No one knew that she had been outside.

When the British went out, they could not find one horse. They looked and looked. They were very mad. But they didn't think to ask Betty what had happened to the horses. Betty was just 13 years old!

Fort Henry

One day, Betty's father said, "It is not safe here, Betty. You must go to live with your uncle at Fort Henry."

So Betty went in a coach to Fort Henry. It was a small fort set deep in the woods.

People lived in houses near the fort. They worked on the land, making room for gardens and cows and more houses. Little by little, they turned the woods into farms and homes.

Betty stayed with her uncle for four years. She liked living in Fort Henry.

One day, British soldiers came. All the Americans raced to the fort. The British tried to get into the fort, but they could not. The Americans had food, water, and gunpowder. Betty knew that they were safe.

But the British soldiers did not stop trying. Day after day, they fired at the fort. Day after day, the Americans stopped them.

Many days went by. The food started to run out. Then one night the Americans saw that they were low on gunpowder.

Betty's uncle said, "If we do not get more gunpowder, the soldiers will take this fort."

The next morning the soldiers fired on Fort Henry. The Americans did not fire. They had so little gunpowder!

Then Betty's uncle shouted, "I know where to get some gunpowder. It is in my house. But that is outside the fort!"

Many people shouted, "I'll go get it!" They talked and talked about it.

At last Betty said, "Let me go. I can run fast. And you are all needed in here."

The Americans talked some more. Then at last Betty's uncle said, "Yes, go, Betty. Keep low and run fast! The soldiers are sure to fire at you."

The Americans opened the fort's door a little. Betty raced out. The soldiers did not fire at her. When they saw her, they laughed in surprise.

Betty stayed low. She raced to the house. She got the gunpowder. She started to run back.

Then the soldiers saw what she had. At once they started to fire. The Americans fired back. They tried to help Betty. Betty raced across the land to the fort.

Then she was back at the fort. The door was open. She was safe inside!

The Americans were happy. They had the gunpowder they needed. They fired at the soldiers. Soon the soldiers gave up trying to take the fort. They went away into the woods, and they did not come back.

And that is how Betty Zane, an American girl, saved Fort Henry.

Paul Bunyan

Do you know about Paul Bunyan? Paul was the first logger. Of all the people who worked in the woods of America, Paul was the greatest. He was the first, and he was the best.

People still tell tales about Paul Bunyan. Here are some of the tales they tell.

When Paul was very young, he was very big. He grew fast, too. When Paul was one year old, he was too big to stay in the house. So his mother put her son's toys and bed outside. Paul liked to sleep out-of-doors. But one night he got a cold.

Now when people get a cold, they sneeze. Right? Paul sneezed, too. And what a sneeze! People for miles around jumped out of bed at the noise. "Must be thunder!" they said. Paul's sneeze knocked down all the trees on a hill five miles away. That is how big Paul's sneeze was.

Paul grew and grew. Soon his bed was too small for him. His father made a bed as big as a boat for his son. He let the bed float on the sea. That way, Paul was rocked to sleep at night by the waves. It was nice. Paul liked it a lot.

Then one night, he did not sleep so well. He rolled and turned in bed. The bed rocked up and down. The waves around him got bigger and bigger. Then a giant wave rolled over the land. That wave made the Great Lakes. You can still see them today.

As Paul grew up, he liked to walk in
the woods. One day, he saw a giant ox
in the snow. That ox was so cold that
she had turned blue. Well, Paul helped
the ox to get better. But the ox never
did get back her color. So Paul called
her Babe, the Blue Ox. Babe was big,
too. She helped Paul in his work.

One day, Paul looked at the woods. He said, "I think I'll be a logger." Loggers were people who went into the woods and cut down the big trees. Then the logs were pulled to a sawmill. The logs were cut up into wood. People used the wood to make houses and many other useful things.

Paul cut down many trees in the West. You can tell that he did. Some places in the West do not have many trees. They have lots of grass and farms but not many trees. Those places are called the Great Plains. Paul made them.

One time, Paul and Babe were pulling logs out of the woods. They pulled the logs up a road to the sawmill. But that road turned this way and that. It turned around and around.

That road turned so many times that it took people three days to walk two feet on it. A woman once got lost on that road. By good luck, she ran into herself going the other way. The two of them worked together and got off the road at last. That was some road!

Paul looked at that road and said, "I have to do something about this." He roped Babe to one end of it. Then he said, "Pull, Babe!" Babe pulled hard.

All at once, he heard a noise like thunder. Babe had pulled all the turns out of the road! After that the road ran in a straight line just as far as the eye could see.

At times, Paul did not pull the logs out of the woods. If he could, he used a river. He put the logs in the water and let them float out of the woods.

One day Paul had a lot of logs. He wanted to float them on the river. But the river was going the wrong way.

Paul didn't care about that. He put all the logs in the river. Then he got on one of them.

He pushed, and all the logs floated the way he wanted. But he did have one bad time. He had to work really hard to get all those logs up over Niagara Falls!

Now you know some of the tales they tell about Paul Bunyan. But did you know what some people say? They say that the tales about Paul are not real. Now what do you think of that?

Oh, Susanna!

I come from Alabama, with my banjo on
    my knee;
I'm going to Louisiana, my true love for
    to see.
It rained all night the day I left, the
    weather was so dry;
The sun so hot I froze to death.
    Susanna, don't you cry.

Oh, Susanna! Don't you cry for me;
I've come from Alabama with my banjo
    on my knee.

188

I had a dream the other night when
    everything was still;
I thought I saw Susanna a-coming down
    the hill.
A buckwheat cake was in her mouth, a
    tear was in her eye.
Says I, "I'm coming from the South,
    Susanna, don't you cry."

Oh, Susanna! Don't you cry for me;
I've come from Alabama with my banjo
    on my knee.

Map It Out!

A map is a drawing of a place. A map can show where there is land and where there is water. It can show many other things about the place, too.

A map can tell about the whole world or a small part of it. This map shows one neighborhood.

190

A map key helps you read a map.
Why do you think it is called a <u>key</u>?

Key

 school    house    zoo

 hospital    store    park

Try This

Use the map and key to tell if each sentence is <u>true</u> or <u>not true</u>.

1. The school is on Beckwourth Street.
2. The zoo is on Bunyan Street.
3. Susanna Drive crosses Bunyan Street and Beckwourth Street.
4. The map shows three parks.
5. Stores are on Zane Avenue.

Look at this map of a railroad.
Follow the train as it goes from
Booktown to Surprise City. Tell the
right place or places.

1. The railroad line starts at _____.
2. The first stop is _____.
3. The Grand Mountains are across from _____.
4. To get to Bridgeville the train must pass the towns of _____ and _____.
5. The stop just before Surprise City is _____.

Magic Tales

The King Who Was Polite

GRETCHEN SETS OUT

Gretchen and her mother lived in a little house. They had a small garden. They had no gold, but they were happy with what they had.

Then one summer no rain fell. No plants grew in the garden. Gretchen's mother looked out the window.

"Daughter, we have no food," she said. "We're sure to die this winter."

Now, Gretchen was a bright girl.
She said, "I have a plan, Mother.
This very day I will go out into the
world and make my fortune."

With that, she set off down the
road. As she walked along singing,
she met a woman.

"Where are you going, so happy and
bright?" asked the woman.

"I'm off to make my fortune," said
Gretchen with a smile.

"And how will you do that?" the
woman asked.

"I'm not sure. But I'm sure that I will," said Gretchen.

The woman smiled. "I like to see a girl so happy," she said. "So I'll tell you what to do. Up this road lives a proud king. He's very proud and very, **very** polite. Tell him what tale you will. He will never say to you, 'That's impossible!'

"The king will give a bag of gold to the one who can make him say, 'That's impossible!' You can try three times. If you cannot do it, off comes your head."

Gretchen laughed. "That is just the thing for me," she said. "I am very good at making up tall tales. I'll tell him one of my tales. He will say, 'That's impossible!' And my fortune will be made. Thank you, kind woman."

Gretchen bowed to her. Then, singing, she went on up the road until she came to the castle. She knocked at the door, and who came to open it but the king himself!

"I'm here to try for the bag of gold," said Gretchen.

The king smiled very politely. "Do
come in," he said. "You can stay in
the castle. Tomorrow morning, you
can make your first try."

"Very good!" said Gretchen.

The next morning, the king took her
outside. He showed her a horse.
"I call this a big horse," said the king.

Gretchen smiled. "Oh, yes," she
said, "it is big for around here. But
back home, we have really big horses."

Then Gretchen told her first tale.

Gretchen's Horse Story

I remember a horse we once had. One morning, I said, "I think I'll ride that horse." I started to climb up on it. I climbed all day. By night, I was only part way up. So I climbed back down and went home to sleep. I spent four days doing this. At last, after five days' climbing, I was on its back.

Just as I sat down, that horse started to run. Before I could stop it, we had run all the way to China!

I called, "Stop!" The horse tried. But it was going too fast. We started to slide. We went all the way around the world. By good luck, we came to a stop in back of my castle.

It took five days to get down from the horse, too. Then my mother said, "Thanks, Gretchen. That horse needed a little run. Some day, I'll let you ride one of my big horses."

Gretchen waited for the king to say, "Oh, come now. That's impossible!" But the king only smiled and said, "Those must be very big horses."

MORE TALL TALES

That night, Gretchen said to herself, "It may not be so easy to get the gold after all. The king really is polite!"

The next day the king showed her some bees. They were big as owls. "I think my bees are very big," he said.

Gretchen laughed. "Oh, yes, they are big for around here," she said. "But where I live we have some **really** big bees."

Gretchen's Bee Story

I remember once we were building a big tower. We were all busy putting up the walls. So we did not see the bee fly down inside. Well, we got the walls up and put on the roof. Then we heard a great buzzing sound. We looked in the tower, and what did we spy? A giant bee, wanting to get out!

What could we do? The doors and windows were far too small. In the end, we had to take the walls down to let out the bee. Then we had to go rebuild the tower.

That bee got out and flew up into the sky. It was so big, it got in front of the sun. It made the land dark as night. Then the bee got lost in the dark. Do you know that that silly bee got lost in its own shadow? It flew around and around for five days. We did not see the sun once in all that time. What do you think of that?

But the king only smiled. "That must have been some bee," he said.

That night, Gretchen sat down to think. She was unsure of what to do next. All at once, Gretchen laughed. "Yes," she said, "**that** will do it. I will get the gold for sure." With a smile she went to sleep.

The next morning the king showed her some big corn plants. Gretchen said, "Oh, they are big, I'll say that. But at home we grow really big corn."

Gretchen's Corn Story

I remember some corn we grew once. It was big. It went up into the sky. Then it went up into the clouds. It ran out of sky and clouds, so it went up into the stars. Why, each night the moon had to stop and duck under that giant corn plant.

One day my mother told me to go up and pick the corn. "At once," I said. Well, I climbed up the steep plant. Soon I was past the clouds. Then I climbed some more. I was up by the moon. That is when I fell.

I fell and fell. I fell feet first for three days. When I hit, I went so deep into the soil that only my head showed. I had to do something, but what? Then I knew. I took off my head. "Run home," I said loudly. "Get help!"

My head was nearly out of sight
when a mean little fox jumped at it.
When I saw that, I got mad. I jumped
up. I ran and gave that fox a good
hard kick. And do you know what
happened to that fox?

It turned into a king! And that
king was **far** more polite than you!

"That's impossible!" shouted the king.

Gretchen laughed and jumped for joy. "You are right," she said. "That it is. And I have won the gold."

Then the king laughed, too, for he liked Gretchen. The king was happy to pay the gold. Gretchen thanked the king and bowed. Then the storyteller set off for home, laughing and dancing all the way.

And that is how Gretchen made her fortune in the world!

The Nightingale

by Hans Christian Andersen

Once, long ago, a king lived in a beautiful castle. All around the castle lay a great park. The park was so big that no one knew where it ended.

Most people came to walk in the park and to look at the beautiful flowers. But some came to listen to the song of a nightingale that lived at the far end of the park. This bird sang the most beautiful song in the world.

One day the king got a book. The book told all about the king's beautiful castle and park. It said, "The park is very beautiful. But the most beautiful thing of all in the park is the song of the nightingale."

When the king saw this, he put down the book. "Well, **I** have never heard this nightingale," he said. No one around him knew of the bird, for they never went out of the castle.

"Go and find this nightingale,"
said the king. "Ask it to please come
and sing for me."

The people ran out of the castle to
hunt for the nightingale. They found
the little bird at last, thanks to a
small girl. When the girl heard the
story, she said, "Oh! I know where the
nightingale lives. Come with me."

She took them far into the park.
At last they came to a tree, where a
small brown bird sat.

"Why, it is a very plain little bird," said one of the people from the castle.

"Listen," said the little girl.

Then the nightingale started to sing. Its song was so beautiful that all the people laughed with joy. A man said, "Oh, the king will be pleased."

They asked the bird to come to the castle that very night to sing for the king.

"I will," said the nightingale. "I will be happy to."

That night after supper, the people
waited. All at once the king called,
"Be quiet, all! The nightingale is
here." Into the room flew the small
brown bird. It sat on the back of a
chair and bowed to the king.

"Please sing to us," said the
king. The nightingale started to sing.
And the beautiful song filled the
castle, so that all stopped what they
were doing and listened. As for the
king, he cried with joy when he heard
the beautiful song.

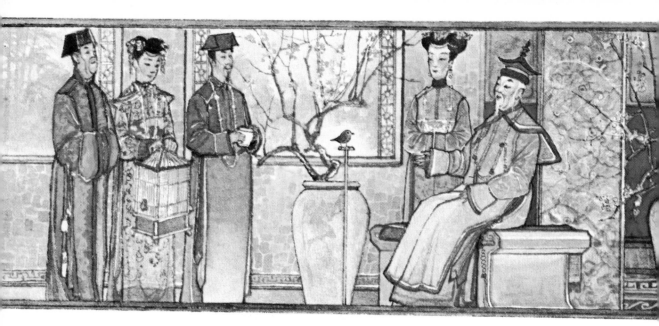

Then the song was over. The king said, "Please stay with us here, nightingale. I will give you a cage made of gold. Three people will wait on you night and day."

"I will stay," said the nightingale, "but not for the cage or the people. You cried as I sang, oh king. I will stay. For now I know that you really love my song."

Each day after that, the nightingale sang. And each day the king's eyes were made wet by the songs of the nightingale.

In this land lived a very bright man. He heard about the nightingale. He said, "Well! I will make a toy nightingale for the king. I will make it out of gold." This he did. When it was made, he put it in a box. He sent it to the king.

The king took the gold bird out of the box. All the people around him said, "It is very beautiful!" And it was. The toy bird was the color of gold, beautiful and bright as the sun.

The king turned a small ring in the bird's back, and the bird started to sing. The bird's song was beautiful. When the song was over, the king turned the ring again. And the toy bird sang the song again.

The bird sang the same song over
and over. But it was a very beautiful
song. And the bird never grew tired of
singing it.

"This is a much better bird for a
king," said the people.

"That is so," said the king. So the
king put the gold bird on the window
near his bed. To the real nightingale
he said, "Go away, plain little bird.
Do not come near me again."

The real nightingale did not say a
thing. It flew up and out the window,
far, far away.

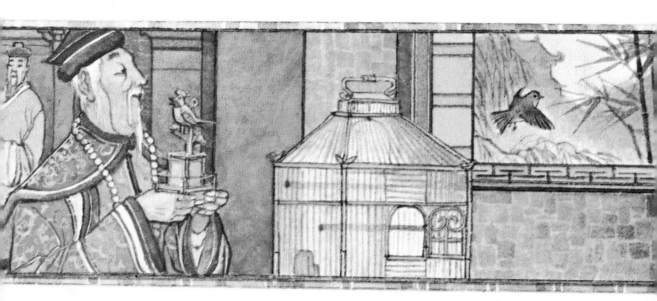

For days and days the king and the people played with the beautiful toy bird. All of them said that the toy bird was **much, much** better than a real nightingale.

One day, as the king was turning the ring of the toy bird, he heard a **crack.** After that, the bird did not sing at all.

The king called in his wise people to fix the bird. At last one man said, "I can fix it a little. But from now on you must not play it all the time. If it cracks again, it cannot be fixed."

After that, the king played the toy bird only one time a year. Once each year he turned the ring on the toy bird. He listened to its beautiful song. Then he put the bird near his bed and waited for a year to pass.

One day the king grew ill. At first he did not think about how he felt. But as time passed, he grew more and more ill. At last he was so ill that he lay down in his bed to wait for the end. One morning he said, "If I do not get well today, I will not get well at all."

His eye fell on the gold toy by his
bed. "Oh, that will help me get well,"
said the king. "The bird's song is
magic. It will make me better." He
turned the ring on the bird. "Sing,
bird, sing," he said.

But the bird did not sing. How
could it? It was only a toy . . . a toy
that had cracked and could not be fixed.

"If I had heard the song, all would
be well," the king said sadly. He fell
back on his bed and cried.

Then, all at once, the most beautiful of all songs filled the room. It was a song about the woods and flowers, about the blue sky and the rain and lightning. It was a song about people working and children playing. It was a song about animals, trees, rivers, and mountains. It was a song that said, "Up! Get up, oh king. Be well again."

The king was filled with joy. He got up out of bed and went to the window. Outside, in a tree, the real nightingale was singing. The nightingale sang, and as it sang, the king grew well again.

"Oh, beautiful nightingale," cried the king. "You have saved me! I am sorry that I sent you away. Come live in my castle again."

The nightingale said, "No. I must live free. But listen, king. I will come to you each night. I will sing to you, only you. Once each day I will sing to you about your beautiful land, and the people, and the world."

"I will listen," said the king.

So after that, the king listened to the song of the real nightingale. He lived for many years. He was a wise, just king, to the great joy of the people.

New Words

PAGES 9-14

Benny
Rex
across
Carlos
him
let's
dig
Ruth
Bobby
Rosa
garden

PAGES 15-19

penny
Ann
grandfather
grandmother
supper
elephants
real
own
note

PAGES 20-24

Andrew
before
bed
skates
bat
ball
neighbor
officer
firefighter
catcher
nice

PAGES 25-30

May
main
quiet
heard
holes
way
bulldozer
long
Ray

PAGES 34-40

wild
try

parts
world
cold
lie
might
food
right
why
brings

PAGES 42-48

pandas
boots
China
older
years
or
roll
faster
sight
teeth
softer

PAGES 54-61

doctor
care
sickest
hospital

monkey
helper
shot
lion
newest
bigger

PAGES 66-69

tools
use
better
how
fastest
peel
workers
deep
useful

PAGES 70-72

hammer
nail
than
feel
hit
hard
head
together

B
C 3
D 4
E 5
F 6
G 7
H 8
I 9
J 0